Clues
to the
Kingdom

Clues
to the
Kingdom

a mystery
BY EDNA
HATLESTAD
HONG

book design
and illustrations by
ollie jacobson jensen

AUGSBURG PUBLISHING HOUSE
Minneapolis   Minnesota

CLUES TO THE KINGDOM
Copyright © 1968 Augsburg Publishing House
All rights reserved
Library of Congress Catalog Card No. 68-13423

Manufactured in the United States of America

This book is dedicated
to
a garland of grandchildren

Krestin Hong

Kevin Elveton

Solveig Elveton

Tait Loe

Sara Loe

Blitz O'Sullivan

May they know the ordinary happiness of the Kingdom of the First Spontaneity—and the extra-ordinary happiness of the Kingdom of the Second Spontaneity.

CONTENTS

Who says there's a crime?

Lord, what was hindermost
in your thoughts when you
said:

I tell you this:
unless you turn around
and become like children
you will never enter
the kingdom of heaven.

Let's turn off the Galilean drivel about
    lilies and sparrows,
        fig trees and vineyards,
            sheep and shepherds,
Jesus, and talk sense—objective, scientific, 20th century
sense. You know very well that when childhood is gone, it's
gone, and nothing on earth will fetch it back.

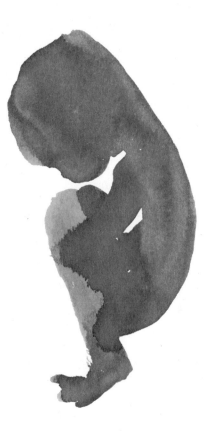

Black strap molasses,
yogurt, geritol,
wheat germ,
Finnish baths,
Turkish baths,
Yogi exercises, calisthenics,
and the whole alphabet of vitamins cannot
fetch childhood back again.

The only way we can turn around—as you yourself put it,
Jesus—is to take a long hard look at existence and crawl
back into mother's womb, curl up in her warm, dark, hidden
uterus and never come out into the cruel world again.

But then they stick us in the nuthouse, plug our brain
waves into the electric socket and shock us back to the cate-
gorical facts:

the graying, receding hairline,
the failing, fading eyes,
the puckering, corrugated neck
—veins slackening, knotting,
arteries corroding, hardening,
stomach sagging, ulcerating,
the tired bowels,
the fagged sex organs,
the arthritic knees,
the ugly corn-fretted feet
where death begins its slow upward creep.

Furthermore, Jesus, you know very well that we resent having childhood taken from us. It seems to be a mark of our humanness to resent it.

Does the sea gull moan its moulted feather
and the old moose buck the loss of passion?
Does the tomcat wail for the madness of former moons,
or the horse for its skittish, coltish days?

But we who are supposed to crown your almighty Father's creation are always trying to be what we were, always trying to invent ways to recapture our lost childhood. It seems to be a mark of our lostness!

Lostness?

Do you mean that we have lost more than childhood?
As if childhood were not enough to lose!
As if the long decay that is adulthood
were not enough to bear!

You, Silent One, you let me rant on and on, and yet you say nothing! You know that I know what you mean—that you desire the life-wearying human body to stop contemplating the child's exuberant body. You ask the dying human spirit to contemplate the child-spirit again. You ask the human spirit to learn again

the child's secret,
the unique grace of childhood,
the mystery of the Kingdom.

Lord, in the common parlance of the day a mystery means a crime.

A crime? Are you saying that there was a crime? Or is?

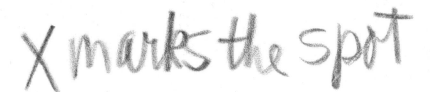

X marks the spot

Lord, you also said:

> Let the children come to me;
> do not try to stop them;
> for the kingdom of God belongs to such as these.
> I tell you,
> whoever does not accept the kingdom of God
> > > like a child
> > will   never   enter   it.

Who taught you your blunt speech, Lord?

Chaste, unsophisticated Mother Mary,

spinning plain prose as honest as her homespun?

Guileless, honest carpenter Joseph,

paring and truing his words

as he planed his wood?

But Lord, good Lord, what have we done with your plain-spoken words, your tough words, your teeth-chattering words?

> Listen, you veterans of childhood,
> you are exiles,
> > outsiders!
> Do you hear?
> Do you understand?
> *You have lost a kingdom!*
> And the mystery of how to get back in
> *I have locked within the child!*

We have taken these words of yours which do not spell comfort, no matter how we jumble them, and have made them into a eulogy of childhood—

> a darling package deal
> wrapped in little-boy-blue,
> dusted with talcum powder
> and fastened with a pink safety pin.
> When a Kingdom has been lost—
> and if not lost, in jeopardy!
> A Kingdom so precious—

well, Lord, if I remember right what once I knew so well and have too long forgotten—you yourself put the price on it, wrote it not in dollar signs but in blood.

Lord, compared to your earth-ranging, man-tracking Spirit, I'm only an amateur detective, but if you don't mind, I would like to carry on a private investigation (by your leave and with his professional help).

There seem to be two mysteries here:

(1) The mystery of how we lose, wander from, go astray from, fail to keep, fail to win—the Kingdom.
(2) The mystery of how to find, find again, and keep if we have found—the Kingdom.

There's a bewildering array of suspicions and suspects. All I know for sure now is the ABC of the case.

A B C

(A) The Kingdom is infinitely precious, and we are infinitely precious to the Kingdom.

(B) You are not profoundly scandalized by our losing or jeopardizing the Kingdom—
you are profoundly grieved.

(C) You are not demanding perfection of us. You demand that we accept the Kingdom
like a child.

    Whatever

            that means!

Lord,
I have a feeling
that a red balloon and
a smudged window pane
have more meaning in this mystery
than a
blood-stained razor
and a sinister finger print.
An abandoned toy truck in a sandbox
will provide more clues than
an abandoned get-away car.

The Lost Identity Card

You work fast, Lord. Yesterday the doorbell rang. I opened the door, and there stood your clue-giver, Child, Kristin her name, three years young—my granddaughter. (Her sly parents hid behind the lilac bush.) "Here I am!" she cried. "Here's Kristin!"

> Here I am,
> Only I,
> I alone.
>
> There is no other I.
> There never was.
> There never will be.
>
> I happen but once,
> never before,
> never again.
>
> Look at me!
> Who do you see?
> Me—Kristin!
>
> I'm only three—
> But I am!
> I am who I am!

And there she was indeed—a once-only being who had already found her once-only self.

> Three years ago Creation spoke:
> Let there be Kristin,
> and Kristin was—and is—a new-
> > fledged reality,
> > > original,
> > > unique,
> > > complete,
> > > absolute.

All sorts of begetting and begatting went on to make Kristin—I had a hand in the production myself. And yet, in spite of biochemistry, despite ancestral pedigree, Kristin is not a soiled copy, a shop-worn ditto, a fourth or fifth slightly revised edition of the same.

Lord, is this your first clue to the crime of losing a Kingdom? Are you telling me that I have lost my ID card—the true identity, the unique self you gave to me?

> Could *I* stand in the door of the Kingdom
> with all the aplomb of Kristin in my doorway
> and say:
> > "Here I am!
> > Here is the self you gave to me,
> > to no other but me,
> > to become"?

Ah, my Lord, I seek clues to the Kingdom, and you give *me* the third degree! I hear your question:

Why are you not fully and completely your own self? It isn't like the human brand of queries:

>Why are you not your peerless grandfather?
>Why are you not your illustrious ancestors?
>Why are you a disgrace to the family?

>May I ask a question, Lord?

>How does one get back the ID card
>one has carelessly thrown away?

1198

$3655\frac{1}{2}162$ 1

the numbers game

Kristin did not stand in my doorway and say:
"Here *we* are!"
WE,
the family,
the clan,
the generation,
the race,
the gang,
the team,
the fraternity,
the firm,
the corporation,
the public,
the majority,
the party,
the state,
the nation.
The child said:
I.

Kristin did not say:

> Here's a social security number.
> Here's a punched hole in an IBM card.
> Here's a statistical item in a census poll.
> Here's a baptized Christian digit in the church files.

The child said:

> *I.*

Kristin did not say:

> I am more than you see.
> There's ever so much more of me.
> Don't look at me.
> Look at my public image,
> the one my hired image-maker made.
> There you will see the me I want you to see.

The child said:

> *I.*

Kristin did not say:

> I am a zero that adds to nothing,
> a flub, a flop, and a failure—
> the stupid, blundering miscreation
> of a tenth-rate Junior Fate,
> discarded before I was ever born.

The child said:

> *I.*

Lord, have we lost the Kingdom because we have forgotten the simple Kingdom arithmetic

which reveres

one,

which does not add and subtract, multiply or divide

one?

Because we have forgotten your sublime arithmetic which is like none

of the world's arithmetic?

In the world:

1000 is more than 1.
1 is less than 1000.

In the Kingdom:

1 is more than 1000.
1000 is less than 1.

Well, well, it's happened again! The clue I pounced upon grows barbs and fastens in *my* proud flesh! The auditor who came to examine the Kingdom accounts is audited and found hiding in the crowd! Adam hid from you in the bushes, and I, Lord—I hide from you in the crowd.

They say one can't teach an old dog new tricks.

Is it possible, Lord, to teach an old cipher
in an anonymous entity she calls society

old truths,
simple elemental truths
she knew *as a child?*

MEN BEHIND MASKS

All day long I wondered what clue you were trying to communicate to me, and finally—when I leaned over her crib to say goodnight, it crashed through the barricade of my old stale opinions. All day long Kristin's Sunday face has been no different in its
> sunniness and cloudiness,
> its gleefulness and poutiness,
> than her
Monday-Tuesday-Wednesday-Thursday-Friday-Saturday face.
> Why,
> I asked
> myself,
are adult Sunday faces, adult vacation faces, adult retirement faces, and sometimes preachers' Monday faces—
> *sad faces?*

Strange I never thought of it before—*because they have lost their functions!* And if, perchance, we wear our function faces fiercely on Sunday and vacation days, it may well be that we are using Sundays and vacations to make ourselves function better when we function. Ah, Lord, I suspect we sometimes even use *you* to procure and insure well-being and success in our functions!

Child's brain has not yet oozed into his fingertips and muscles.
Child's will has not yet congealed into his habits and duties.
Child has not yet put on the stereotyped face of function.
Child's meaning is not yet synonymous with his doing.

Child is not what he does.

Kristin's face is still her own—not the teacher or the preacher mask, the manager or the director mask, the wife, husband, and parent mask. Kristin's face is the true, transparent face your Father gave to her.

Lord, if we may come back into your Kingdom

we may feel for a time like a nun

who somehow has wandered into a nudist camp.

All those naked faces—those faces stripped of their function masks—

may shock us—

until our eyes become accustomed to the

radiance

of the peeled pith of self.

the disfigured image

Kristin wrecked Kevin's 4-lane superhighway
                    (accidentally),
and Kevin threw sand in Kristin's eyes.
Kristin scratched Kevin's face
                    (intentionally).
Kevin went home crying,
and his mother came over fuming.

                                        After Kristin
went to bed tonight I went to my shelf of poets,
                    where I always go
                    when I get a cinder in my eye
                    and a sliver of ice in my heart.
The poem leaped out at me from printed page.
                    Aha, I thought, another clue,
                    and where I least expected it!

The Kingdom of God

by
Francis Thompson

The angels keep their ancient places;
Turn but a stone and start a wing!
'Tis ye, 'tis your estrangéd faces
That miss the many-splendoured thing.

'Tis *we* and our estranged faces,

'tis *I* and my estranged face—

that miss the many-splendored thing!

Lord, I'm more than embarrassed!
Why did you let me spout about pseudo-selves and function masks—
    as if all we have to do to reenter the Kingdom
    is rip off the masks and
    present the transparent face
    of childhood?
    When you know what you have always known—
    that the face of man, though peeled of masks,
    is smeared, smirched, stained, defamed.
    In the uttermost brightness of your Kingdom
    not even Child does shine!

Sometimes when a cinder
turns into an image of horror
burning the eyeball
and a sliver of ice into a glacier
freezing the heart's blood,
poets do not suffice, and so I
went to your Word, the first book of Moses,
commonly called Genesis.

> So God created man in his own image.
> In the image of God he created him.

Once upon an eon when Creator God bent over to look into the face of man, Creator God saw *his own reflected image*. When God bent over once again and looked into man's face he saw no reflected image—he saw the mark of Cain.

> Dachau and Hiroshima—
> A livid scratch on Kevin's cheek.

> God searches an old woman's face
> to find his likeness there and sees. . . .

> Have mercy, Lord!

> Have mercy!

FUGITIVES
WITHOUT
PASSPORTS

Today I called Kristin's parents and asked if she could stay another week. (I did not tell them I was investigating a crime and that their daughter was providing clues thick and fast!) They sounded lonesome—reluctantly granted me a week's grandmother-indulgence. "Well—maybe—as long as she's happy."

Happy? Kristin is happiness incarnate! I have a feeling her happiness, Child's happiness, is connected somehow with the Kingdom. To that end and for my dossier I translated two of Kristin's "Happy Songs" (the songs without words her being hums and he who has ears to hear hears).

Song I

I have a little circle
that goes around with me.
I'm always in the middle
secure as I can be.

The roundness of an apple,
the fullness of a pear,
accompany their center
like the circle which I wear.

It cribs me like a blanket,
my personal universe
eternally surrounds me,
its happy nucleus.

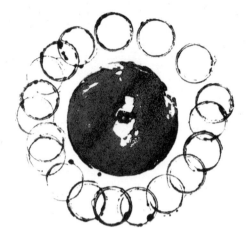

Song II

Ring-a-ding-ding!
Ring-a-ding-ding!
        Ringed by stars and sun and sea,
        Everything, everything rings around me!
                Rings around me!

Swing-a-ling-ling
Swing-a-ling-ling
        The lovely things in my galaxy
        Swing round and around about me!
            Round about me!

Spring-a-ling-ling
Spring-a-ling-ling
        The lively things that dance with glee
        (Sunbeams and such) dance around me,
              Dance around me.

Sing-a-ling-ling
Sing-a-ling-ling
        The red, red robin in the cherry tree
        is lyrical for me, for me,
            Is lyrical for me!

Ah, Lord, the trust and security of those who are loved is like a passport stitched into a secret pocket!

And we—modern man—

we who have lost faith and the Kingdom—

what are we but fugitives without passports,

homeless in space,

small ugly specks on a giant cogwheel,

doomed to infernal circles!

The great tri-impersonals—

blind fate,

blind force,

blind fortune—

washed us up on the beach of time,

and therefore we are what we are—

metaphysical bastards.

We huddle together in our alien universe

wherever the whirlwind flung us—

alone, afraid, superfluous, marginal.

We clutch the rim of the hoop with breaking, tearing fingernails, wheeling, whirling, turning, spinning—ringing around the emptiness, the stupid, impersonal emptiness.

Lord God, how does a fugitive without a passport, how does a man without a Kingdom, come to wear once more the child look, the proud look, the buoyant look of the divine right of citizenship—

in the Kingdom?

Murdering
the
Kingdom
English

Lord, it wasn't until I was through being angry that I realized you had slipped in another clue. While Kristin napped this afternoon, I watched a TV program—one I had watched many times before, but it never affected me the way it did today.

They put kids in a box, in a bright lighted box in a darkened room. They put words in their mouths—cheap, worn-out words, slightly soiled. Hearing their own words in the mouths of innocence they laugh loudly—like monsters.

Lord, your Father created man a subject,

and we have let ourselves become object—

and insist on making our fellow men into objects!

Child is supremely a subject, and we make even Child an object!

Lord, you are a teacher. You know the Kingdom grammar.

How can you stand to hear us

murder the Kingdom English in this way?

A teaspoon of man's liquid lust spills

and spawns

Child.

Or man intends Child,

makes Child the object of his selfish

drives, his selfish ambitions and greeds:

> the fruit of his survival urges
> deductible dependent on his tax forms
> consumer for his products
> citizen for his states
> cannon fodder for the world's armies
> one more political vote
> one more inductee for our military
> one more convert for our crusades
> one more card in the church files
> one more shopper, buyer, client, patient
> one more charge-a-plate
> one more credit card.

Lord, Lord, why do you tolerate such misuse of divine grammar? Why don't you break the ruler over our heads? Why don't you raise your voice in anger—

> "Listen, you numbskulls—
> you seniors and elders!"

Ah, but it is not your way, Lord! It is not the way of one who treats another for what he is—a subject!

Lord, these nights, while Kristin sleeps, I'm reading everything you said. I hang upon your words like a ship-wrecked sailor who has not heard human speech for endless years. Tonight you said—sorrowfully—(Matthew conveyed your message):

You did not enter yourselves
And you hindered those who were entering.

Ah, there it is! There is the utterly, utterly degenerate un-grammatical misuse of Kingdom grammar—for which not even being stood in a corner is sufficient punishment—not even being stood outside the Kingdom!

> 'Twere better that a millstone
> be hung about his neck
> and that he be sunk
> in the depths of the sea.

Why did you think of a millstone, Lord? Because it's apropos—a heavy object for us who make objects of created subjects?

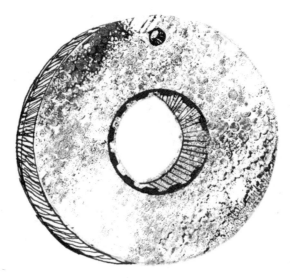

the ancient
grudge

I took her to the arboretum today—thought I'd introduce her to the flora and the fauna. She skipped ahead of me along the path, greeted a bluejay with delighted laughter. Without knowing its name—either the familiar or the formal—she greeted it as if it were an old acquaintance. She touched a cluster of harebells as tenderly and tranquilly as she sometimes strokes my face. Hugged the adolescent birch as if it were her favorite babysitter.

I *introduce her* to your Father's creation? Lord, I get your clue! Child is at home in creation. Pink sand, tinted sea shells, dappled pebbles, sparkling rain beads, muzzling kittens, nudging puppies, furry caterpillars—know and are known by Child. And all this juice and all this joy, all this grace and favor which you created in Child to celebrate the radiant mystery of creation, all this we lose in *fresh fall,* inheriting the ancient grudge.

Man desires to possess and monopolize creation, and it will not. Man seeks to seize and dominate creation, and it becomes his enemy. Man demands sum and substance of creation, and it envelops him like an ulcerated stomach. Child runs toward your creation with open arms, and we hurl ourselves at your creation as if we were greedy suckling pigs and the world a brooding sow.

Therefore, Lord, to set the record straight I place in the files—the grimly glutting files where I am recording man's alien touch—two sad and silly songs.

Song I

Child likes the cow all red and white.
We like the milk check with all our might.

Child likes little piglets, so pink and so sweet.
We like porkchops and pickled pig's feet.

Child likes the hens, some brown, some white.
The money the eggs bring is our delight.

Child likes the Black Angus who thinks he's boss.
We like his steaks with Worchester sauce.

Child likes the ducks with their Quack, Quack, Quack.
We like them best on the barbeque rack.

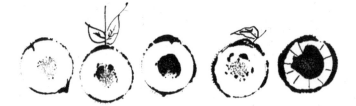

Song II

Ripe fruit that falls untasted,
    wasted.
Maids that can't be lured to bed
    unwed.
Sincerity, integrity
if they have no utility
for our economy.
Crippled horses,
Old decrepit people.
The dead
once their wills are read.

the jammed communication system

Lord, today I think I saw the antenna
you stationed on Kristin's north pole
where her wheat-straw hair meets
in a funny little swirl.

It's a most acutely sensitive instrument.
When glad surprises surge in from all sides, it sways madly.
> It trembles to weather,
> it trembles to fields,
> it trembles to sea sand,
> it trembles to most anything.

And when she simply stands and stares at nothing in particular, her antenna is no doubt sending her a very delicate communication.

Lord, I wonder if we do not begin jamming your communication system when we begin teaching Child to pray? Thank you for the food we eat. Thank you, God, for bread and meat. As if bread, meat, and potatoes were the only thank-worthy gifts! I wonder if the antenna would go dead if we taught Child to celebrate your whole wonderful system of communication? For example, Lord—

TOUCH

Thank you for cobwebs that lightly touch my face
and gently remind me of soundless things
like spiders and butterflies
(crickets and bees don't need to spin reminders).
Thank you for the cool squishiness of mud,
the roundness and hardness of pebbles,
the steep upness and downness of hills,
the rippled firmness of wave-washed sand,
the cool surprise of raindrops,
the kiss of sun on bare skin,
the warm red feel of garden-ripe strawberries,
for foam-feel,
my pony's velvet nose,
my dog's tongue which tells my hand and face he loves me,
and the gift of tender touch you gave to me
to say it back to him.

As a matter of fact, Lord, I don't think you threw thunderbolts at Adam on his second day out of dust when you said: "Good morning, Adam, how do you feel?" and Adam answered, "Great, Lord, I feel great! And thanks for the feel of Eve. Thanks, Lord, for shaping Eve different from me!"

Or was Adam a poet? Did he write a Song of Adam in praise of Eve—only the publishers rejected it and took Solomon's instead:

> Behold, you are beautiful, my love,
>   behold, you are beautiful!
> Your eyes are doves
>   behind your veil.
> Your hair is like a flock of goats,
>   moving down the slopes of Gilead.
> Your teeth are like a flock of shorn ewes
>   that have come up from the washing.
> Your lips are like a scarlet thread,
>   and your mouth is lovely.
> Your cheeks are like halves of a pomegranate
>   behind your veil.
> Your two breasts are like two fawns,
>   twins of a gazelle,
> that feed among the lilies.
>   Song of Solomon 4:1 ff.

Ah, Lord, I have come to see that when we
see and are seen,

hear and are heard,

touch and are touched,

smell and are smelled,

taste and are tasted,

we are more present in

spirit, and spirit is more present in us. The senses you created in us *are on the side of spirit.*

Lord, creation-callousness

is not separate from Kingdom-callousness!

Blunting, dulling, and deadening

the senses of Child,

killing the sentient Child,

is not only a sin against nature—

it is a sin against the Kingdom!

Lord, where does guilt stop?

Is there no boundary to sin?

a mouldy crust of bread

Today, Lord, a giant jet crashed in the Near East. There were no survivors. Our Air Force bombed a village in the Far East, and two African countries broke off relations. A child in New York was raped and murdered, and an old woman in Seattle was bludgeoned to death and robbed of $3.67.

> And yet, Lord,
>
> Kristin is lying up in her bed singing!
>
> Is this a clue to the Kingdom—or not?

Yes, yes, I know—

life tastes good to Child;

the knobby, parched, and puckered apple of life tastes good. I know, too, that Child skips lightly up the ramp of time and does not look down, does not see the dizzy chasm, the appalling abyss, the nightmare pit. The fates hurl their atom bombs, and Child tosses them back. They fall lightly, like balloons on a breathless day.

> The earth shudders,
>
> and Child leaps in ecstasy.
>
> The universe rocks;
>
> Child turns handsprings.

Each night sleep comes on tiptoe to Child, sweeps up the loose ash of the day and scours the grudge-smudge away.

Each morning Child
cups his hands and re-
ceives life, thumb-rim
full, and lets fear slip
through his little fin-
gers.

And we, Lord? We wake from troubled sleep, loath to accept the dubious gift of a new day. And while we lie abed, reluctant to get up, our ancient fears and hostilities drip their distilled poison into the cup which sleep has emptied. Life has a daily-sameness taste, like a damp and moldy crust of bread left over and forgotten.

Lord, if this is a clue, I challenge it! I'll grant you that compared to buoyant, bouncy Child we live a ghastly, ghosted life. I'll grant you that Child relishes the whole wheat bread of daily life and that we ask our bread to be buttered with fresh churned butter, spread with homogenized honey, and curse it when expectation becomes stale disappointment.

But Child's spontaneity, Lord,

is born of innocence and ignorance.

"Heaven lies about us in our infancy,"

and the landscape of childhood is fair indeed

   for the Child lucky enough to be loved.

But then comes hell,

the scales of innocence flake off.

and Child begins to see the humanscape.

Like a little child, Lord? What do you mean?

Once we have tasted sin's subhuman stew, how can life taste good again?

You said it yourself:

"I am the bread of life."
"I am the living bread which came down from heaven."

How does one get this bread, Lord? How does one *get you?* Please don't give me all the stilted answers to all the questions I never asked and never cared to know and had to memorize, word for word!

Ah, was that it, Lord?

I never asked and never cared to know.

Cross examination

Speaking of questions, Lord,
somebody remarked today
that a person gives his true self away
in the questions he asks.
   Splendid!
I shall herewith record in my dossier and
place in my fat files
on "The Case of the Lost Kingdom"
the questions I have heard
this week.

The Questions Women Asked

Where have you been?
Who was there?
What did you eat?
What did they wear?
What did they talk about?
He's marrying *her?*
What does he see in her?
Don't you think it's a sin?

The Questions Men Asked

Why should I stick my neck out?
What's in it for me?
How much did it cost?
What make did he buy?
Where can I get it for less?
Who's ahead?
What's the score?
What's Anaconda today?

The Questions Kristin Asked

Where does your lap go when you stand up, Grandma?
Why doesn't day stay?
Where do the stars stay all day?
What do angleworms eat for breakfast?
Why don't big people turn somersaults?
Why don't they even try?
Do fish talk to each other?
What is the chipmunk saying?

Lord, need more be said? Child's questions smell of life; man's—of death.

> When does the moon dim
>
> and the machine begin to shine?
>
> When does the mockingbird grow still
>
> and the cash register begin to sing?
>
> When does the ocean stagnate
>
> and the stock market become majestic?
>
> When does creation play out
>
> and things become exuberant?
>
> O Lord, reply, reply!

But you don't reply! I pile up evidence against Man, against the whole stinking human race—and you silently hand it back to me—silently. But your very silence cross-examines! Why do you have to make everything so squirmingly personal?

Kristin has been here two weeks now, and in all that time she has never asked, "Grandma, what time is it?"

Lord, why is it Child never asks: "What time is it?" until we adults teach him the question—and then he never ceases to ask the time.

For Child the ticking of a watch is a gay and marching rhythm, a disembodied sound, unbuttoned from the past and future, not yet attached to urgent schedules. Child's now is fluid, flows on and on and on, full of always, always now. For Child time is unforgettable time in which he forgets time.

Is this why Child just sort of flows into your Kingdom—right through the walls of that Kingdom, while we who have lost the Kingdom beat, bang, and batter at the gate:

> Let us in!
> Let us in!
> Before it's too late!
> Time is running out!

Is this why we troubled transients in time cry for yesterday, wait for tomorrow, and despise today—the disease that is our present?

The pendulums swing,
the hour hands crawl,
the minute hands walk,
the second hands run,
and what do the clocks say to us adults?
"We number the days,
the days are numbered,
time is running out.
The past is gone,
the present is going,
the future is not yet.
Now is vacant,
volatile,
a desperate interim.
We punctuate
the emptiness,
we regulate
the void. . . ."
That's what the clocks say to us veterans of childhood!

Lord,
what a terrible conception of time and eternity we adults have!
For us eternity is tomorrow and tomorrow and tomorrow,
some other then,

        some other there,

                lasting forever,

                        arriving never.

How infinitely remote!
How devastatingly lonely!
I do not want to sit and wait

        and wait

                for such a future!

I get your clue, Lord! Child's first timeless time is a moving picture of eternity! Your eternity broke and breaks into time. You, the I AM who was, is, and ever shall be, offer yourself to me *here,* where I am, *now,* when I am what I am!

tell me the exact time it happened...

We had a visitor today—
a female relative,
an unctuous dame.
Lord, I'm a woman,
but I can't bear women who,
when they speak to children,

               butter their voices,
               pitch them sweet,
               chirp and twitter,
               tweet, tweet, tweet.

"Honey," she bleated, and her buttered popcorn words
left oil-smears on the freshly rain-washed air.

"What are you going to be when you grow up?"

           "I think—"
           said Kristin gravely,
           with a taking-everything-
           into-consideration look,
           "I think that I'll be—ME!"

Me

I almost said (until I understood that she was just another clue!):

"Can *you* tell me the precise time
when Child comes *to be?*

At 5 A.M.,
with the sunrise of sex?
At 7 A.M.,
when he flips the tassel of his board?
At 10 A.M.,
when he goes to bed with bride?
Come, tell me please—
when is the moment *to be?*"

How utterly absurd to say that Child is preparing for life, that Child will become somebody *someday* (perhaps the minute he gets his first pay check?)! Being is not a finished product—wrapped, dated, and delivered at a proper time under specific conditions. Being is a nucleus unfolding, a never-happened-before God-given self growing up to the Light, finding its true self.

Child is being *on the way* NOW,
concretely full of personal being NOW!

Lord, it looks as if losing the Kingdom has something to
do with our thinking of Child as ə
rib-bound, bone-braced, skin-snug,
pint-proportioned container,
deficient in time,
devoid of being,
into which we the venerable ones
pour content.
It has something to do with our thinking of ourselves as
gargantuan gallon urns,
replete with time,
exuberant with being,
pouring the superfluity of our toomuchness
into Child's hollow container.

Thanks, Lord! There's consolation in this clue as well as
knuckle-rapping and conceit-spanking! You've waited long
for me, Lord, but I—I don't have to wait to enter the Kingdom until my virtues weigh 775 pounds, my nobility is 10
feet tall, and my self-confidence is bright orange!

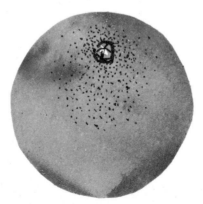

the break-through

"Where have you been?"
(The female visitor to Kristin,
helicoptering home from secret worlds
and ampler orbits.)

Said Kristin: "In the big green forest—
and a cub bear ate
my popsicle."

Lord, I had to do it—I spiked her lecture on truth with a Pilate thrust:

"What is truth?"

Of course we got nowhere. She hit me over the head with her tidy tenets, and when I grabbed her confounded concepts and proceeded to undress them, take off their wrappings and their trappings, she got so very embarrassed at their nakedness she fled.

Naked truth,
    peeled and pared,
    husked and hulled—
Lord, isn't that the way
    truth dwells in Child
and Child dwells in truth?

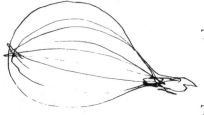

Truth is what is interior in Child—
    naked,
    integral,
    and incarnate.
Truth is what is exterior in Child—
    manifest,
    transparent,
    luminous,
    and unmistakable.

Child carries his interior truth
    in front of him like a
    bright red flag.
Child wears his interior meaning
    on his face,
    and we read its gospel truth
    word for word.
Child is the truth he knows,
    and this is truth—
    becoming and being
    the truth one knows.

Is this a clue to Kingdom loss—that we have long since ceased in all humility to become and to be the truths we talk and write about?

Lord, I just had a vagabond vision! I saw a procession of scientists, analysts, theologues, pedagogues, Hebraists, Sanskritists, philosophers, lexicographers—in solemn progression, marching to the Kingdom. Stopped at the gate, not even the weight of the tons and tons of volumes and tomes won their way in. And a barefoot boy in jeans darted between their legs and trotted right into your Kingdom and didn't even have to hold out his hands to show that they were clean!

Ah, but this was only just another of my vagrant, irreverent visions, and my fumbling for truth brings only partial truth. Who is able to be the truth he knows! Not even Child can be that! Forgive me for romanticizing, idealizing, sentimentalizing Child!

Lord God Almighty, All-knowing, All-wise, Omniscient, Infinite, and Eternal One—I don't want crumbs and scraps of truth! I want the truth, the whole truth, and nothing but the truth!

God, when we humans have dealings with each other, when we want to affirm something as true, we give our word for it. That's all I ask, God—your word!

O Christ, how blind can I be! You were—you *are* that word! O Word of God, mystery revealed, truth made manifest, Word made flesh—and we crucified you!

Escape Artist

That was a great break-through last night, but somehow clues are still breaking into my thick skull! An unmistakable one today—

> Kristin walked through a wall
> so solid, strong, and stubborn
> that Houdini would have blanched and bolted.
> But not Kristin!
> She walked right through that pitiless barrier
> as if it were child's play—
> and not a hair of her head was rumpled!
> Went through it as if she did not see it,
> but it *is* there,
> and no one knows better than you, Lord,
> that it is there!

> > Higgledy-piggledy,
> > potpourri,
> > alla-podrida
> > gallimaufi,

without once having heard of caste, class, or race, interracial harmony and desegregation, interracial unity and integration—or, for that matter, the American dilemma, prejudice and discrimination, segregation and recrimination, the Ku Klux Klan—little white Kristin tripped to town, skipping with Nat who is chocolate brown.

White and black,
yellow and brown,
dance together
in the children's town!

And your higgledy-piggledy Kingdom, Lord,
belongs to such as these,
who walk through all the color, caste, and class barriers,
and quietly split all the iron curtains
we adults raise.
Your higgledy-piggledy Kingdom, Lord,
belongs to such as these,
who see every living thing
just as it is,
just as Adam saw the world—
with no prejudices, no anxieties, no fears,
no formerly formed associations.
Your higgledy-piggledy Kingdom, Lord,
belongs to such as these,
who know the truth, and the truth possessed
makes or keeps them free.

Liberty? Freedom?
Lord, the clue hit a snag!
I have a feeling
that the liberty of your Father's children
is more than skin deep and boundary wide.

I suspect that the best way to escape the man-pound
where humans who have lost their freedom are impounded
is to dig deep down into the narrow place which is our
prison.

Set me to digging, O Heavenly Hound,
tenaciously and joyously,
hot on the heels of freedom,
and scattering catchwords and slogans
as a dog scatters dirt in a hedgehog hole.
Lord, I'm warning you!
I'm going to grab hold of this freedom-mystery
and hang on as tenaciously as a bulldog,
wrestle with it as stubbornly
as Jacob with his angel!

The Terrible Risk

The green balloon, clenched and clutched, broke with a loud POP.

Kristin wailed her loss. The red balloon, floating from open palm, curtsied, hitched a ride with the willing west wind, and soared away. "Look at it go!" yelled Kristin. "Just look at it go!"

Very well, Divine Levity,
you Favorable Wind who lift man to the Kingdom,
what symbol of freedom rides a red balloon?
What will you say to one who was born to freedom
and has lost her family rights,
her Kingdom privilege?

      What will you say to us who have set cautious limits
      to our lives,
      measured safe and easy goals,
      barricaded ourselves behind normalcy,
      shut out the unpredictable,
      and resigned ourselves to things as they are?
  What will you say to us who have sold our freedom to
the great god Public Opinion?

      What does the morning paper think?
      What does the TV commentator think?
      What do the pollsters think?
      What does the computer think?
      If the computer says it's so—it must be so!

71

What will you say to us who are slaves to our virtues as
        well as our vices,
thralls of our barren correctness and rigid perfection—
we who comfort ourselves with our pet prejudices,
mouth them as an infant sucks his pacifier,
and achieve the same glazed contentment.
We, the shoulder-shruggers, the so-whaters,
mouthing our stale cliches:

I'm only human.

I don't have what it takes.

Whatever will be
        will be.

That's the way the cookie crumbles.

We, the unconditionally conditioned ones:
        Don't blame me
    —blame my mother—
that possessive domineering female
who dowered me with her dour genes;
that rigid hypocritical Mother Church
who filled me with morbid guilt feelings;
my silly, senile Sunday school teachers
who converted me into a Christian snob;
    my dear, doltish Alma Mater
who reconverted me into an intellectual snob.

O Spirit of Freedom, what will you say to us who hide the horrifying state of our unfreedom in forlorn anxieties and frantic hustle and call this progress?

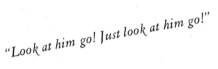

"Look at him go! Just look at him go!"

Aha! I get it!
You—almighty, all-competent, all-powered God.
you who created a whole universe,
every infinitesimal part of which
is dependent upon your will—
yet—you—powerful, tough Omnipotent,
you made the most fragile of all things—
a free being!
You cut the umbilical cord of dependence
and gave man the terrible freedom
to walk alone!
You did not even put him in a walking harness!
You removed your hand gently,
and when you saw him walking alone,
you had the omnipotence,
you had the grace to say:
"Look at him go!
Just look at him go!"
Oh, incomprehensible mystery, that you, the Omnipotent,
made me to be free! Oh, inconceivable marvel, that you, the
All-powerful, grant so much liberty to me that you ask me:
"Will you have me or not?"
—and wait for my answer!

The Malignant Climate

"Come, Kristin,"
I said this morning, "let's go down by
the creek and see if the asters are blooming.
Maybe the elderberries are ripe and the adolescent
frogs are jumping.
   Please come."

Kristin, free by the grace of God and carrying her gift lightly within her interior self, put her hand into mine. We two absolutes, separate and free, joined our hands, locked our fingers, and walked together, linked and inseparable.

Lord,
isn't that exactly what you want—
free beings
related
in freedom?

Is there any sight more beautiful to you in heaven and on earth than free beings choosing one another, associating with one another, working with one another, playing with one another—

in freedom?

Isn't that the secret of all truly creative human relationships? Isn't this the secret of the tragedy of no-relationship?

Cribbed in laxity, full of hostility, flaunting authority,
20th century man thinks to be free means:

        "I against all,

        all for me,

        I for no one,

        no one but me."

And in the very detachment he demands

    (thinking this is freedom!),

he builds the walls of his prison,

isolates himself in the terrifying loneliness

of solitary confinement!

Lord in your higgledy-piggledy Kingdom freedom-attachment, and capacity for freedom-capacity for attachment.

      In your crazy Kingdom arithmetic

        it takes

         2

        to make

         1—

two free and loving solitudes to make one strong, healthy, indissolvable relationship.

$$1+1=1$$

To grow like a tree, upward ascending, Child needs a climate advancing its being. Lord, Lord, I am beginning to see the dimensions of the crime! Child, neither philosopher nor theologian, grasps spontaneously at your gift of freedom. Child, creature of space and time but intended for the Kingdom, craves relation to these three: your holy Trinity, your creature man, your creation.

All Child wants is what Child needs—the favorable climate where he can learn to trust and love these three: your holy Trinity, your creature man, your creation. Child remains free to the precise extent he is able to love these three: your holy Trinity, your creature man, your creation. If Child, whom you give to us in trust, receives of us a climate hostile to you, hostile to man, hostile to nature, *how can Child come into the Kingdom?*

The absence of thee! O lethal legacy! Crime that outherods Herod! I see what you mean, Lord, about

> visiting the iniquity of the fathers
> upon the children
> to the third and fourth generation
> of those that hate me.

THE NIGHT WAS DYED ITS DEEPEST BLACK

Star light,

Star bright,

First star I see tonight.

I wish I may,

I wish I might,

Get the wish I wish tonight.

We lay on the knoll in the apple orchard, riding the crest of the spinning earth, watching the stars come out, and wishing on every star. Finally, when it looked as if someone had sifted granulated stars all over the ceiling of the world, Kristin cried,

"Grandma! Grandma!

A sky full of wishes!"

Lord, how many of your children went to sleep tonight under a sky full of hope? How many are sleeping this night the deep and dreamless sleep of those who hope? How many will rise refreshed tomorrow, renewed by the sleep of hope?

How many, O Lord, toss and turn this night under a darkened sky, waiting without hope for morning? How many lie staring in the dark while the blind moles of despair tunnel deeper? How many will rise tomorrow more exhausted in body, mind, and spirit than when they went to bed?

Lord, I'm beginning to see that hope is the oxygen of the Kingdom and that the mood of despair shuts out the air of heaven!

Hope lives in Child a fragile flower, subject to frost and the desert winds. Basically and fundamentally, and all unaware, the infant child wishes and hopes and wills—spontaneously and immediately—what you, Lord, will infinitely:

affirmation and acceptance,
response and love.

If Child's world neither affirms nor accepts, responds to nor loves, the stars go out for Child, one by one, all over the sky. And that's where the real troubles start—back there with the death of hope in the heart of a little child!

Apathy and indifference,
absence of feeling,
absence of concern,
non-involvement,
negativity and hostility,
pessimism and defeatism,
futility,

paralysis of will, the all-pervading despair—all begin with the death of hope in the heart of a little child.

Lord, has there ever been an age like this when the intellectual elite, the arty esthete, and the insolent beat find life
at the core a nauseous bore, a slatternly whore, and fall in
love with despair? I went to your Word to see, read the
Old Testament Preacher of Pessimism, read the plaintive
Poet of Lamentations, but there I found only the *right kind
of despair,* the despair which says:

> I find no hope in me;
> therefore I hope in thee for me.

Lord, I see, I see!
The Kingdom hope is not
>   a silly grinning hope,
>   a happy-ending optimism,
>   a pill-produced brighter mood,
>   an "everything will turn out in the end" hope,
>   a day-dreaming, self-glorifying hope.

The Kingdom hope is greater than Child's rosy-cheeked hope,
which is a
>   blithe sense of the possible,
>   a gay faith in being able,
>   the spontaneity and imagination to support both,
>   and the resilience to bounce back
>   when it is dashed down.

The Kingdom hope is the stripped-of-all-earthly-hope hope
>   —the hope which says:

> I find no hope in me;
> therefore I hope in thee for me.

slow strangulation

A very subdued Kristin today. Tonight at bedtime it came out.

"I don't like your house so much any more, Grandma."

And so I called my son, told him love had not run out but home-longing had filtered in.

Frankly, I'm puzzled, Lord. Is this a clue to Kingdom-loss? Child loves spontaneously, and spontaneous love is—well, if not fickle, frangible! And the trouble and the tragedy of what passes for love these days is that it remains childish love, spontaneous love, subject to change and therefore inconstant.

Ring the bell madly,
I've fallen in love.
Toll the bell sadly,
I've fallen out again.

Lord, when you said that we cannot enter the Kingdom unless we become like children, did you mean that we are *to love like a child?*

Kristin tonight
expressed her loneliness and love
for the two
you in your first and foremost love
gave to her to love love into her.
Into her what, Lord?

Into her *ableness* to love!
O Lord, that's it! That's it!

The love-*ableness* of the Child-spirit

is what you want us to recover!

Love-*ableness* resides in Child as a love-need of the spirit, a deeper love-need than the love-need of the body. Love-need in Child is a perfect vacuum, offering no hindrance whatsoever to love. It inhales love as naturally and freely as voided lungs inhale oxygen—and needs love just as much!

And if the nucleus of love,

the love disposition of Child,

cannot ascend to the Light,

it descends to the Dark.

If it cannot love,

it must hate.

Sinned against and sinning, love-*ableness* in Child becomes an imperm-e-ability, a crippled capacity, a cancered lung, silted with sin and exhaling hate and hostility. What resided in Child as simple childish openness now is closed-up-ness, an inability to relate in love.

You are taking away my clue-giver, Lord; you must think the mystery is practically solved. Are you going to leave unanswered my last question:

Can the sinning

love each other?

Spirit of Love,
did you tenderly hold old John's hand
and literally escort it across the scroll,
tracing the utterly simple words
of that utterly extraordinary message:

> We love
> because he first loved us?

Ah, I shall memorize that first letter of John's word for
wonderful word!
Crucified Love,
you who made visible what love is,
your love is perfected in us.
This is the miracle
        —and the task!
The cancer of hate *can* be eradicated and the love-*ableness*
of Child restored, the love-vacuum *can* be filled—with love!
Men *can* love again like children who are loved first,
like children whose initial, original love-*ableness*
is nurtured and not disabled!

Kristin went home today,
promising to return "tomorrow."
Am I forlorn?
Am I bereft?
Am I downhearted?
Lord, I am so *up*hearted
that if I spread my sail I shall float out the open window
and shoot upward toward the moon,
to the other side of the moon.
Have you abrogated the law of gravity, Lord?
No, 'tis only I that float.
The paper weight is still sedate!

Is this your bonus, Lord? Your divine dividend? I merely
asked that you roll the stone away, and you have levitated
me as well!

Child I cannot be—joyous Child, effortless delight, rap-
ture for just being.
Child lives in the First Spontaneity,
in the Land of Tra-la-la,
under a pastel sky.
But I have seen sin;
I know and have seen
the jungles, swamps, and deserts
of sin.

I know and have seen the ugly crevices and craters
on the lovely face of life.
But you, O Divine Juggler,
you have lifted me to the other side of sin,
to the Kingdom of the Second Spontaneity!

We poor mortal beings are always searching for the button of happiness. Some few sift the gray matter. Some many reconnoiter in the sex organs. Others hunt among the taste buds. Others probe with needle and alcohol. But your Kingdom-man, Paul, put the finger on the button right away.

> Law came in
> to increase the trespass,
> but where sin increased
> Grace abounded all the more.

You took me far out, deep down, and under my quiet and cultivated and always dignified rebellion. You showed me my nothingness—but not to make me despair—only to show me the greatness of your grace! Lord, I bless your rod!

Your clues piled sin upon sin, trespass upon trespass—until I wondered if ever I could laugh again. But then you laughed into my being with your grace.

Jubilantly,
from the healed, reconciled, and redeemed
depths of my being,
JOY
wells up again!
Spontaneously—
and like a child!

Only now it is on the other side of innocence and ignorance, the little-girl-pink and the little-boy-blue, on the far side of the Land of Tra-la-la, on the far side of the Land of Ish, the cinder in the eye, the bitter black vomit. Now my joy is in the Kingdom of the Second Spontaneity,

where the redeemed being

cries HOSANNAH!

Hosannah to God in the highest!

My soul trembles with astonishment. Is this really me?

Lord God, the winter is past, and the staff of my old age has sprouted sticky green leaves!

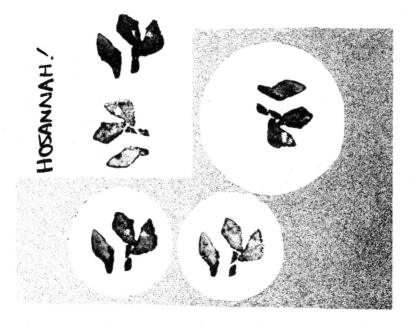

the case is closed.

Lord,
I don't quite know what happened yesterday.
In quieter, calmer, retrospect, it seems
that I just shut my eyes, whispered,

> "Ready or not,
> here I come!"

—and jumped.

Today I'm not sure whether I landed in the Kingdom or the Kingdom landed in me!

Is this what they call "the leap of faith"? Is this what you called "being born again"? Is this being born into the mystery you have locked within Child?

Sleeping and waking, I now know grace—your free gift to my free being. Sleeping and waking, I now know how to accept the gift—*like a child!* Sleeping and waking, I now know what I have accepted like a child:

the gift of life
  (in the Kingdom),
the gift of the true self
  (the whole of me, the good and bad, calmly possessed)
the gift of the forgiven self
  (the bad forgiven),
the gift of love-vitality
  (the good energized because you loved me first)
the gift of Now
  (George MacDonald calls this "the holy carelessness
  of the eternal Now"),
the gift of grace
  which Child grasps spontaneously
  and Man appropriates paradoxically).

It seems the case is drawing to a close—not that all the mysteries are solved—the mysteries of life after death and of resurrection, for example. But who wants to know all the mysteries of sometime when the meantime is jampacked with mystery revealed! O Triune God, the drama and the mystery you reveal in the tiny enclosure of a moment, a split second! Oh, the mysterious synthesis of all that coexists in the split second that is Now! —My need and longing for you, your giving yourself to me in Christ, your Spirit pouring into me. My spontaneous response—my turning around and embracing in gratitude the little bit of world you have given me to love.

> *All of it—*
> not picking and preferring
> what is worthy of my love
>> (how can I,
>> when *you* did not!).

"See what love the Father has given us, that we should be called children of God; *and so we are . . . ,*" said that Poet of the Kingdom, John. "Beloved, we are God's children now; it does not yet appear what we shall be, but we know that when he appears we shall be like him." It has truly happened—! When the Lord God bends down to see his image, he'll see himself in me—in *me!*

> And so we are
> God's children NOW.
> This, then, is the mystery,
> this is the miracle,
> this is the Kingdom Come!

Thank you, Lord.

Thank you, Kristin.

Lord, all that time Kristin
was her grandmother's playmate,
did she know that she
was your collaborator?

THE AUTHOR

Edna Hatlestad Hong is a wife and mother of eight children. She has found time during her busy schedule to write two other books—*Muskego Boy* and *The Boy Who Fought with Kings*. She and her husband, Dr. Howard Hong, are co-translators of *For Self-Examination* by Søren Kierkegaard. Mrs. Hong is also a frequent contributor to religious publications. She has written stories for *Christmas: An American Annual of Christmas Literature and Art,* and articles for the *Lutheran Teacher* as well as poetry for *The Lutheran Herald, The Lutheran Standard, Response,* and *Arena.*

The Hongs have lived in Northfield, Minn., since 1939 except for spending two years in Germany working with refugees and two years in Denmark where they translated Søren Kierkegaard's journals and papers. Dr. Hong is a professor of philosophy at St. Olaf College, Northfield, the same school from which Mrs. Hong graduated magna cum laude with a B.A. in English and History.

THE ILLUSTRATOR

Ollie Jacobson Jensen is an art instructor at South St. Paul Senior High School, St. Paul, Minn., and a part-time lecturer in art education at Augsburg College in Minneapolis. She has illustrated three other books for Augsburg: *Home Is Where God Is, The Little Liturgy,* and *Whose Zoo?* Her illustrations frequently appear in curriculum and education periodical materials of the American Lutheran Church.